I Am
Respectful

by Sarah L. Schuette

Consulting Editor: Gail Saunders-Smith, Ph.D.

Consultant: Madonna Murphy, Ph.D.
Professor of Education,
University of St. Francis, Joliet, Illinois
Author, *Character Education in America's
Blue Ribbon Schools*

Pebble Books

an imprint of Capstone Press
Mankato, Minnesota

Pebble Books are published by Capstone Press
151 Good Counsel Drive, P.O. Box 669, Mankato, Minnesota 56002
http://www.capstone-press.com

1 2 3 4 5 6 07 06 05 04 03 02

Library of Congress Cataloging-in-Publication Data
Schuette, Sarah L., 1976–
   I am respectful / by Sarah L. Schuette.
   p. cm.—(Character values)
   Summary: Simple text and photographs show various ways children can
be respectful.
   Includes bibliographical references and index.
   ISBN 0-7368-1442-6 (hardcover)
   1. Respect—Juvenile literature. [1. Respect.] I. Title. II. Series.
BJ1533.R4 S38 2003
179'.9—dc21   2002000531
                        30303000316770

Note to Parents and Teachers

The Character Values series supports national social studies
standards for units on citizenship. This book describes respect and
illustrates ways students can be respectful. The images support
early readers in understanding the text. The repetition of words and
phrases helps early readers learn new words. This book also
introduces early readers to subject-specific vocabulary words, which
are defined in the Words to Know section. Early readers may need
assistance to read some words and to use the Table of Contents,
Words to Know, Read More, Internet Sites, and Index/Word List
sections of the book.

Table of Contents

4

I am respectful. I treat people the way I want to be treated.

I respect myself. I take care of myself.

I respect the earth.

I recycle newspapers.

I show respect to other people. I shake hands with the people I meet.

RESTROOMS

♿ MEN

12

I show respect by waiting patiently for my turn.

I whisper when I am in the library.

Library Book Return

I am careful with things that belong to other people.

I thank people
who help me.

I am respectful and kind.
I think about the feelings
of other people.

Words to Know

feeling—an emotion such as happiness or sadness; people who are respectful care about the feelings of other people.

kind—friendly, helpful, and generous

recycle—to use old items so that they can be used again in new products; people recycle cans, newspapers, and plastic so that they can be made into new products.

respect—to believe in the quality and worth of others and yourself; people who are respectful treat others the way they would like to be treated.

thank—to tell someone that you are grateful; people who are respectful thank others for favors they have done for them and for nice things they have said to them.

treat—to act toward people in a certain way; respectful people treat others with kindness.

whisper—to talk very quietly or softly

Read More

Agassi, Martine. *Hands Are Not for Hitting.* Minneapolis: Free Spirit, 2000.

O'Neal, Ted, and Jenny O'Neal. *Respect: Dare to Care, Share, and Be Fair!* Elf-help Books for Kids. St. Meinrad, Ind.: Abbey Press, 2001.

Raatma, Lucia. *Respect.* Character Education. Mankato, Minn.: Bridgestone Books, 2000.

Internet Sites

Adventures from the Book of Virtues
http://pbskids.org/adventures

Respect
http://library.thinkquest.org/J001709/
thinkquest_values/2respect/respect_frameset.html

What Is Respect?
http://kidshealth.org/kid/feeling/emotion/
diversity_p3.html

Index/Word List

Word Count: 88
Early-Intervention Level: 9

Credits
Mari C. Schuh, editor; Jennifer Schonborn, series designer and illustrator;
Gary Sundermeyer, photographer; Nancy White, photo stylist; Karen Risch;
product planning editor

Pebble Books thanks the North Mankato Taylor Library in North Mankato,
Minnesota, and the Distad family of Mankato, Minnesota, for assistance with
photo shoots.

24